Cocktails at Midnight

by
Paul Doherty

ISBN: 978-0-6459286-5-5

Special thanks to Karin Ravazdy for her editing and wording,

RACK & RUNE
publishing

Published by Rack and Rune Publishing
rackandrune.com
email: info@rackandrune.com

Chapter 1

The sun was shining though a cold wind blew across London. Winter had almost arrived. Hercule Poirot sat behind his polished walnut desk, eagerly going through mail that had just been delivered. He was hoping for a new case to solve. He needed to re-charge those little greys cells. Then he saw it. The envelope was elegant with discreet gold trim, one word engraved on the front. Poirot stared at that word. Squinting through the pince-nez on the end of his nose, that word said *Styles*. Poirot's hands trembled just for a second then he slowly opened the envelope.

The card read, *Monsieur Hercule Poirot, you are invited to Styles Manor House for Cocktails at Midnight. Be there by 11.30pm, this Saturday night*. Poirot's little grey cells vibrated for Styles Manor House was the scene of his first murder case, many years before.

At the same moment in Baker Street, as she had done one thousand times before, Mrs Hudson carried a tray up a steep flight of stairs. The tray held a steaming teapot, two cups, matching saucers and two plates of crumpets with strawberry jam and cream. Leaning against the milk jug were two envelopes. Holding the tray in one hand she slowly opened the door at the top of the landing. She whispered 'Gentlemen,

1

Styles

I have morning tea for you.'

Dr Watson sat in a wing back chair by the fireplace and Sherlock Holmes stood near the bookcase, lighting his pipe. Dr Watson said 'Argh! Crumpets! Wonderful Mrs Hudson'.

Holmes glanced at the tray, 'They look like two impressive envelopes you have there?' Mrs Hudson put the tray on the table, handing an envelope to each of the men. She nodded, then quietly left the room. Both men's eyes were transfixed on the one word on the front of the envelope.

Watson cried 'But he is dead! Holmes, it was a miracle that you survived going over those falls with him.'

Sherlock tapped the envelope on the end of his prominent nose. 'Yes, my dear Watson', he explained. 'Maybe there were two miracles.'

Watson ripped opened his envelope. 'Preposterous!' he cried, 'Cocktails at Midnight, at Styles Manor House.' Holmes, picking up his violin, started to play a mournful melody. The image his mind conjured up was not that of Styles, but rather, of his own true nemesis.

In the foyer of one of London's most renowned Hotels sat a robust man reading his paper. A white gloved purser carried a burnished tray approached, calling out, 'Mr Bulldog Drummond!' The man put down his paper and waved him over. Putting a tip on the tray, he accepted the elegant envelope. The card inside conveyed his invitation to *Cocktails at Midnight, at Styles Manor House*. Drummond, who had just arrived home from New York, ran his hand through his thick hair. 'Who in the hell knows I am here?' he whispered to himself.

In the quaint village of St Mary Mead, the postman arrived at the gate of a beautiful old cottage. 'Ahh! There you are', he exclaimed, as Miss Marple's head popped up from behind a rose bush.

'Oh, Henry', she smiled, 'you have some mail for me? That envelope looks very elegant'. Opening the envelope, she read the invitation on the card, *Styles, Cocktails at Midnight*. As the bell from the Anglican church, rang across the village of St Mary Mead, thoughts raced in Miss Marple's brain.

Across the Channel, Jules Maigret, Commissioner of the Parisian Prefecture de Police, looked down from his office window. Light rain fell on the grey streets of Paris, but Maigret's mind was elsewhere. He held a letter from London, saying, *Styles, Cocktails at Midnight*. He sat down at his desk and picked up the phone. 'Operator put me through to London please. It is an emergency.'

On Saturday night, at fifteen minutes before the appointed hour Holmes and Watson's taxi pulled up at the front of Styles Manor House. They were greeted by Gufferson, the butler. 'Please enter!' he formally invited with a bow.

Walking into the parlour they were shocked to see all the World's greatest detectives gathered in one room. Poirot sat on the sofa next to Miss Marple. At their side were Jules Maigret and Bulldog Drummond. Holmes' face remined unreadable,

'Good evening gentlemen', he said slightly nodding his head. Looking serious, the others silently nodded their heads in acknowledgement.

Gufferson opened two large doors in the adjoining wall, gestured with his gloved hand, ushering them through. Poirot knew this house well. It brought back many bad memories. Entering a large dining room, the detectives sat at the table, in the places indicated with their place cards. Holmes sat at the head of the table. Watson was to his right, then Bulldog Drummond. To his left sat Hercule Poirot, Miss Marple and then Jules Maigret.

The burning logs in the fireplace radiated a comforting heat and a handsome clock ticked on the mantle. The dial said ten minutes to midnight. Gufferson holding a large facetted decanter poured a libation into each crystal glass. 'Gentlemen and my lady', he soberly warned, 'you are not to drink until the clock strikes midnight'. Watson and the other detectives looked at their glasses and contents with suspicion, but Holmes' face never changed.

There was a knock at the dining room door. On opening, the detectives were greeted by a tall, thin man standing in the doorway, holding a satchel. Dressed in black, his sallow face was expressionless. He walked into the room, standing beside Holmes. In a soft voice, he said, 'I am from Murray & Blinkhorn Solicitors and I have been engaged to gather you all here tonight.'

Holmes said abruptly, 'Who is your employer, may I ask?'

'Well, that is strange" he answered, 'it was all organised by correspondence.'

Remaining expressionless, Maigret asked, 'And who are you, Murray or Blinkhorn?'

The man gave Maigret a hard look, 'Blinkhorn', he replied.

Blinkhorn walked to a side table, picking up a large, beautifully carved ebony box and placed it on the table in front of Holmes. Taking a key out of his vest pocket, Blinkhorn placed it on top of the box. At that moment, the clock chimed midnight. All the detectives stared at their cocktails. Holmes held up his hand, shouting 'No one drink'! No one touched their glass. Suddenly, the dining room doors burst open. Standing in the doorway was Inspector Lestrade and two London Bobbies. Behind them was an Inspector from the Parisian Police Prefecture and an Inspector from Interpol.

'Nobody move!' Lestrade shouted, 'we have the whole place surrounded.' Seeing Holmes and the other detectives his face dropped becoming sullen in disbelief. He said to Holmes in a high pitched tone, 'The crown jewels have been taken.' Then to Maigret, 'The Mona Lisa has been stolen.'

The Interpol Inspector added, 'The Banque of Belgium has been robbed', then looking at Bulldog Drummond he gasped, 'the same has happened in New York.'

Finally, Lestrade looked at Miss Marple, 'The famous bell from St Mary Mead's Church has disappeared.'

'What', she cried, 'that bell is almost as old as England itself.'

Lestrade then said, 'We were informed that the Den of Thieves who carried out these robberies, would be here tonight.'

A big smile came across Lestrade's face, 'What have you got to say about that now, Mr Holmes?'

Silently Holmes took the key from the box in front of him, and unlocked it. To everyone's surprise, like a jack in a box, the top flew open and a ghastly figure popped out. It was dressed in black and in each hand, it held two flags, one saying *Check* and the other, *Mate*. All the detectives looked at each other and in unison exclaimed, 'Moriarty!'

Holmes looked behind him for Blinkhorn, but he had disappeared. They had forgotten about him. Watson gasped 'He has to be here somewhere. He cannot just disappear in a room full of people.'

Hercule Poirot rose and walked to the mantelpiece. 'I know this house very well', he exclaimed. Touching a carving beside the mantelpiece, a small panel opened in the wall, just large enough for one person to fit through.

Holmes smiled, 'Well gentleman, the game's afoot.'

Chapter 2

Pensively standing near the window, Sherlock Holmes looked down onto Baker Street. He held a handsomely carved, ivory Meerschaum pipe. Savouring a deep puff of the fragrant tobacco he thought about the previous night's mystery at Styles Manor House.

All the other detectives had joined him at 221B Baker Street. Watson was seated in his favourite wingback chair. Monsieur Hercule Poirot sat primly on the sofa, Miss Marple perched next to him. She stared at Bulldog Drummond moving around, observing the contents on Holmes's cluttered table, idly picking up a Persian slipper containing a strong smelling tobacco. Putting it back on the table he knocked over an African spearhead ornament with a clatter.

All eyes fell on Bulldog who just shrugged. Turning around from the window Holmes gave him a quelling look, then resumed staring out the window. Inspector Jules Maigret admired Holmes's splendid bookcase. There was even a book on *The Soils of Great Britain*. 'All this information at the touch of a finger,' he thought, 'luxury, sheer luxury'.

There was a knock at the door and Mrs Hudson carried in a large tray containing a teapot, cups, saucers and plates of

crumpets with jam. Watson cried out 'Splendid, Mrs Hudson!'

Nodding at Watson she placed the tray on a table, quietly leaving the room. Holmes didn't even turn around; he was still looking down onto Baker Street. A large black limousine slowly drove past. It stopped within Holmes's view. He could see a man sitting erect in the back seat, dressed in black and Holmes was sure he was looking up at him. The car smoothly drove off. The number plate struck him as strange. It read *XYZ*! Before he could think any more, there was a knock at the door and Mrs Hudson showed Inspector Lestrade into the room.

'Ahh, what news do you have for us?' asked Holmes.

'Harry Houdini has disappeared,' Lestrade answered.

Watson laughed 'Well that's what he does.'

Lestrade looked Watson in the face. 'No Doctor Watson. Houdini and his wife have been missing for three days. He and his wife, Bess are supposed to be performing at the Palladium Theatre tonight, but like I said there is no sight of them.'

Smiles appeared on Holmes's and the other detective's faces. Lestrade and Watson looked at them baffled. 'You see,' explained Holmes, 'Houdini is the only man who could get into those banks and unlock the safes'.

Lestrade was aghast 'You mean to say he is working with these criminals!'

Before Holmes could answer the door flew open and standing there was Harry Houdini himself! The great detectives were surprised to see him but were more aghast at his appearance.

His clothes were torn and tattered, his shoes were caked in mud. Looking dazed and weak he fell forward into the room. Bulldog Drummond caught him and carried him to the sofa. Doctor Watson examined their visitor. 'He is completely exhausted and has been probably drugged with opium.' Sherlock Holmes' eyes widened, lips curling upwards with delight.

Houdini gasped 'They have Bess and I don't know where I escaped from, or how I ever got here.' He then passed out.

Looking shocked, Miss Marple exclaimed 'Well we certainly have a mystery here, my friends.'

Holmes took a small penknife from his waistcoat pocket, and scraped some particles of mud from the soles of one of Houdini's shoes. Jules Maigret handed him the book on 'The Soils of Great Britain'. Nodding Holmes walked over to his microscope, placed the soil onto the surface of a slide and slid it beneath the lens. After examining it he studied the book Maigret had given him. He then announced with a touch of arrogance 'Well lady and gentlemen, it's from Essex.'

Lestrade bellowed 'How in blazes did he get here?'

'Precisely my dear Lestrade,' Holmes replied.

Looking delighted, Hercule Poirot gently patted his moustache and said, 'Well my friends, we are going back to Styles.'

Chapter 3

After carefully examining Houdini, Doctor Watson peered over his halfmoon glasses and proclaimed "He needs complete rest. He is drugged and exhausted. I don't know how he managed to find us. We can put him into my bedroom." Bulldog Drummond picked him up, slinging him over his beefy shoulders in a Fireman's hoist and followed Watson into his bedroom before gently placing Houdini on the bed. After covering him with a quilt, the men quietly left the room.

On returning to Sherlock's study, they heard Lestrade stating "I'll have my men go straight to Styles Manor House."

Holmes held up his hand to slow the proceedings down and said "Now, just let your men surround the House, making sure that they cannot be seen by anyone at the house or approaching from the road. Make sure that they are very quiet, and it is essential that they do not smoke any cigarettes so the glow from the match or the lit ends of the cigarette cannot be seen. Tell them to watch what is happening. They are not to apprehend anyone they see entering the house. If they recognise anyone, they should note it in their handbooks. It is a full moon so they should be able to see enough to write.

"Tell them to carefully follow anyone who leaves the

House without being seen. You need to park a number of non-descript cars where they cannot be seen so that they can follow anyone who drives away. They are not to follow too closely behind, so they are not spotted. It's essential that they do not know that your men are there, or the game will be lost."

"Don't you think we should move quickly to catch these fiends and free Mrs Houdini?"

Holmes gave Lestrade a stern look. "They are going nowhere," he responded. "We all know Moriarty, or Mister Blinkhorn as he calls himself, is behind all this. There is a lot more to this mystery to solve at this moment. Like I said, have your men hide and watch the house and report on anything that is happening. We can all rest up here, getting a good night's sleep and tomorrow morning at seven o'clock we will visit Styles Manor House."

"Hmm, maybe you are right Mister Holmes," Lestrade murmured.

"One more thing," asked Holmes, "can you have the number plate of a black Rolls Royce XYZ investigated?

Lestrade looked puzzled, "That's a strange number," he replied. The other detectives all looked at each other, perplexed as well. Lestrade went to the phone in the corner of the room and rang his office. A few minutes later he said to Holmes, a big smile on his face, "The car belongs to a Mister Blinkhorn from Styles Manor House. It appears that he also lives there. Interesting, don't you think?"

The great detectives all nodded, now knowing this Blinkhorn and Moriarty were the same person. Everyone had been certain that Moriarty had previously died, except for Sherlock Holmes who always believed that he was still very much alive. Now his greatest nemesis is back, once again a challenge to his great detective's brain. He almost rubbed his hands together in glee. 'This time,' he thought, 'I have all these other great detectives to help me.' Holmes knew that Moriarty had planned all this as the supreme revenge on him. Moriarty wanted him to not just publicly fail, but to also die. The same fate would also fall on his fellow detectives.

Poirot asked "This number plate, le XYZ, we all know that Moriarty likes to leave clues. This must mean something, so let us put all our little gray cells to work." Nodding to Miss Marple, "Well lady and gentlemen, let us begin."

Holmes walked over to his desk and picked up his violin. Placing the chin-piece of the violin under his chin, but holding the bow idly in his right hand, he looked down into Baker Street at the pedestrians and cars glimpsed through the eddies of swirling mist, his mind was deep in thought. Like the obscuring fog outside, his mind was just the same. 'What had Moriarty's wretched mind planned for them all?' Holmes, despite knowing they were walking into a trap, also knew that this would not stop him. With his whole being, he wanted Moriarty. And he wanted him dead. Permanently dead. Buried at a depth of 12 feet, not just 6 feet, to make sure that he would never emerge again to taunt them. Raising his hand, he ever so lightly drew his bow over the strings of his violin, wincing slightly at the soft screech that it made.

There were only another three sounds harmoniously woven into the ambience of the room, promoting a cozy feeling, belied by the feverish mental activity. One was that of Miss Marple's knitting needles, softly clacking as she worked away on a new jumper she was making for her friend, Isabelle's new granddaughter. This is how Jane did her best cogitating. Another noise came from the crackle of wood, cheerfully burning in the fireplace. The third sonorous noise was coming from Doctor Watson who was asleep in the old leather wingback chair by the fireplace. His snoring harmonised with the crackling firewood so it did not distract the other great detectives.

Bulldog Drummond was a gentleman adventurer and great detective. This case had Hugh puzzled (only the ladies called him Hugh). Miss Marple gave him a sweet smile and he nodded back to her, always the perfect gentleman. This case had them all baffled, what could this XYZ mean?

Poirot was twirling his moustache. His little grey cells were working away at great speed. He thought of his good friend, Captain Arthur Hastings who had been with him at Styles all those years ago. 'We solved that case,' thought Poirot, 'though this time there is the cunning Professor Moriarty to deal with. He is cold hearted as le serpent, and is the master of disguise, so you can never under-estimate him. He never kills anyone himself. His hench men do it for him. He also likes to watch them do his dirty work.

'The tragic thing is that he has a great mind. Possibly equal to Sherlock Holmes himself. They have always had this battle to see who is the best. Ou est le victor, n'est pas? The difference is that Holmes always stands by his fellow man whereas Moriarty wants to destroy his fellow man.

'With everyone believing he was dead all these years it has given him all the time in the world to plan this terrible deed. Who knows what he is leading us into? Moriarty is doing this for revenge on Holmes, we all know this basic fact. So,' he thought gently nodding to himself, 'we must all help him to defeat this terrible monster.'

Maigret sat in silence tapping his beloved pipe, regretfully empty as there was no tobacco in it in accordance with his doctor's orders. 'Those damn doctors!' Jules thought, he loved his pipe and always did his best detective work with it in his hands.

Bulldog Drummond patted his pencil thin moustache and turning to Miss Marple he asked, "Is that St Mary Mead's church bell really that old.?"

Without missing a stich, she replied, "It certainly is Hugh. They say it came from a church in Rome that had been there for hundreds of years before it came to us, many, many years ago.

Still tapping his top lip Bulldog responded, "This situation certainly is a mystery, Jane. There has been no murder as yet, however we do have a kidnapping and seemingly non-related high scale robberies across the world. These have to be connected in some way."

Miss Marple nodded, without taking her eyes off her knitting, "I'll tell you one thing Hugh. This is all to do with Holmes and Moriarty and I believe that Moriarty is merrily leading us all into a trap." They looked over at Holmes who was still peering down into Baker Street. "Furthermore, Holmes knows that this is a trap and is still going to go right into the hornet's nest. He has the beginnings of a plan though and he is still working on it. That's why he has us all waiting until tomorrow morning before we make our move."

Bulldog nodded to her knowing that this innocuous, great aunt appearing, grey-haired, old lady was a genius at studying people. Not just criminal's but people from all walks of life, from house maids to duchesses and in between. 'She had certainly been studying all of us in this very room,' he mused, 'you may think she is concentrating only on her knitting, but I can assure you she has a way of seeing you without you're noticing her. Wherever she goes, on trains or buses, or bookings into an hotel, she studies people around her and how they behave and react to others around them. This woman was an amazing detective. Looking at all these other famous detectives you can see they all have a little device that helps them focus to enhance the power of their deductions. Simple things like a violin, knitting needles, a pipe or even twirling a moustache. Their minds are the most amazing things. Just imagine if you could hear what was going on in these brilliant brains,' he chuckled to himself.

'Then you have the mind of Moriarty, just as intelligent but the only difference is that his mind is full of evil. It is unfortunate that sometimes when you fight evil you have to become evil yourself. You must fight so that you do not to turn to the dark side yourself. Look at the Great War, terrible things were done on both sides. You can only pray that good wins in the end. I know there are people who don't believe in God. I do know without a doubt that this Moriarty is the devil, so God save us all, amen.'

This number plate mystery had them all baffled. Professor Moriarty is a criminal mastermind. He not only ran the underworld from the London docks to the Lime Houses in the back streets of London. He even had connections in the Upper House of Parliament! Yes, his spider web extended all over Europe and even further afield. He loved power and money of which he had several fortunes worth, and if anyone got in his way, he would have them murdered without even blinking. Men, women, even children, terrible things would happen to them.

Moriarty was a master of disguise. He had to be as the real Moriarty, if you were unlucky to ever meet him, would cause you instantly to feel unease and even fear. He is tall, very thin, his cheeks were sunken and grey. His eyes are dark, very dark, very dead, reflecting no emotion. He has a high forehead and short greying, cropped hair. His masterful disguises even fooled Holmes when he played this Mr Blinkhorn. Appearance wise, Holmes is a lot like Moriarty, apart from his eyes, that are full of life, but he too is a master of disguise. They both despise each other and won't rest till one or both are dead.

Holmes knows he must stop this heartless creature. He also knows he must save Harry Houdini's wife, Bess. He realises that she is being used as bait to catch Sherlock Holmes, himself. A small smile appears on his face. Moriarty just doesn't want to kill him, he all so wants to destroy the reputations of the World's Greatest Detectives then he will have the world at his mercy. He has criminals in every country just waiting for his orders before they spring into action. Who knows, there could be another big war coming, bigger than the last war. Just like Moriarty's spider web is growing every day, maybe the World's fate lays in the hands of the people gathered in this very room. Can Holmes and these famous detectives stop Moriarty and his evil disciples from taking over the world?

Lestrade was still sitting by the phone waiting for any news about Styles Manor House. Looking around the room he chuckled to himself at the sight of all the serious faces, all thinking deeply, desperately. 'Despite their brain power, I am the one with all the real power here. I am Inspector Lestrade of Scotland Yard. If anyone is going to catch this Moriarty it will be me. Holmes and his friends are great thinkers, they are great at unravelling puzzles, but it is me and my London bobbies who will make the arrests that lock the blighters up.' Looking over at Watson still snoring in his chair, he thought 'Even I am a better detective than the good doctor. He should just keep to his doctoring and let me do the real detecting work.'

There was a knock at the door. Mrs Hudson came in with a large pot of tea, bowls of hot soup with warm bread rolls on a wheeled cart. Watson suddenly woke and sat up, "I can smell food," he mused, "you, Mrs Hudson, you are a wonder."

She smiled and silently left the room. They all helped themselves to the refreshments except for Holmes. He just filled his pipe with tobacco from the Persian slipper. No one said a word, they just sipped their tea and dipped their crusty rolls in their soup before swallowing them appreciatively. Bulldog Drummond threw a couple of extra logs on the fire to stoke it up. "It must be cold outside now, for it is getting a bit chilly in here." he exclaimed.

As if on cue, Mrs Hudson came back holding enough woolly blankets for them all. She passed them to those gathered, then left the room again. Holmes said, "We should all get some sleep now as we need to arise early before we start heading for Styles." Holmes sat behind his desk, dressed in a long scarlet dressing gown, then wrapping a blanket over himself, he was soon fast asleep.

Miss Marple, Bulldog Drummond and Poirot were sat closely next to each other on the rose-coloured settee. Blankets covered them from chin to toes and soon they were asleep as well. Watson was once again snuggled in his wingback chair by the fireplace, snoring peacefully. Lestrade sat in the other wingback chair on the opposite side of the fireplace staring at the flickering flames in the hearth. Jules Maigret had laid down on the thick rug in front of the fireplace. As an ex-soldier he knew how to pick the warmest and most comfortable spot. He too was soon fast asleep.

Now they are all asleep, dreaming, and their minds fly to faraway places. So, what do these great detectives' minds dream about when they are asleep? Their minds are so advanced in the world of criminology, they know the inner workings of the criminal mind. However, there is only one mind that they are all thinking about now, and that is the mind of Professor Moriarty. They also know he has must have joined forces with an even bigger evil. We may have believed we had beaten them in the great war, but unfortunately the demon is returning from the burning ashes. The enemy may be even stronger this time and with Moriarty on their side, heaven help us. Let's delve into these great minds and see what we can discover.

Holmes dream has him in Switzerland at the top of the Reichenbach Falls. This is where Holmes and Moriarty fought to the death, with both men going over the edge of the waterfall. Amazingly, both men survived. Everyone else believed that Moriarty had died, however Holmes had never really believed this. He knew that one day his arch enemy would return. In fact, he had been waiting for him. In his recurring dream he is fighting him on the top of the Falls where the noise of the water is deafening. He could still hear Watson's voice shouting "Holmes where are you?"

He had dreamt this dream many times over the ensuing years, only this time it was different. In their struggle Moriarty pulls out a German Lugar pistol. Seeing the Luger, he is sure he now knows who is behind all this.

Watson was still snoring, and he also was in a deep dream. He was walking along a lonely, foggy road along the Dartmoor moors. A hound is making a terrible baying sound that could be heard in the distance. The frightening howls echoed across the moors. Even more frightening, he knew that his friend Holmes was out there alone with this devil hound. Watson could see Baskerville Hall in the distance.

Holmes had wanted him to stay there and look after Henry Baskerville. "Look after him with that revolver of yours. Don't let him out of your sight. This is one of the most terrifying cases we have ever worked on," ordered Holmes. That revolver had saved Holmes and himself on many occasions.

Jules Maigret was very comfortable lying on the rug in

front of the fireplace. He was dreaming of his stylish, modern home in Paris. He did not like London at all. The citizens were still little more than peasants, in his opinion. The food, the clothes, the buildings, even the ways of the people, it was so different to those of his beloved Paris. Though, he did like working with these fellow detectives, facing their great challenge of trying to stop this evil Moriarty.

Bulldog Drummond's dream was not pleasant, it was more of a nightmare. He was tied with heavy chains in a pitch-dark room. He could hear noises coming from boats on the river close by. He surmised he must be in the dark and sinister docks on the Tam's River. This terrifying incident had actually happened in the past, and Bulldog was lucky to escape with his life. The nightmare never leaves him, recurring at least weekly or more often when he is under stress.

Miss Marple was dreaming of Saint Mary Mead Church and its famous bell. In her dream the bell was being rung and its peels were ringing across the little village. Her famous case "Murder at the Vicarage" brought back memories to her. She whispered ever so softly "Moriarty you will pay for this."

Inspector Lestrade was standing in the Court room next to Moriarty who was in chains. The great detectives were all in dismay. The media were all saying what wonderful job he had done to catch this fiend. Lestrade had a big smile on his face and his chest was puffed out with pride. He looked over at Holmes with a gloating stare. Holmes glared back with a disdainful look. That look was enough to frighten Lestrade so much that he almost woke out his dream, however his boastful smile remained fixed.

Poirot was walking through Styles Manor House. His good friend, Captain Hastings, was with him. Poirot was telling him that this is a very evil place in itself and not just the people that lived there. "The house is evil too. Behind these walls are a honeycomb of catacombs just like the ones in Rome and Spain. You would not want to know what is buried behind these walls."

Hastings replied nervously, "Hercule I think we should leave this house right now. I am not worried for myself though. I believe something is drawing to this evil place."

"You may be right Hastings however you also know that I cannot leave here until I solve this case and catch the murderer." Captain Hasting knew that he could never get his friend to leave this house and he also knew this place would be the end for the great Hercule Poirot.

In Watson's bedroom, Harry Houdini was also in a deep dream. Like his friend Hercule, he also was dreaming of Styles Manor House and his poor wife, Bess. He knew that those catacomb rooms hidden behind the walls were real as he had previously been trapped in them. He knew that Bess was in another room and his heart was breaking as he was unable to find her in this maze. Houdini had used his locksmith tricks to escape captivity and search the hidden rooms looking for Bess.

Sadly, he could not find her and the only thing that saved himself was that he was the greatest escape artist in the world. He knew he needed help and there was only one man that could help him to free Bess. That man was his good friend Sherlock. Houdini knew he had been drugged. He knew there was a lot of people involved in the kidnapping. Despite being drugged and blindfolded he could still hear their voices. The determination of Harry Houdini was stronger than these drugs. There were twelve different voices in his nightmare. Two of them were women and they all could speak English and German. 'I must reach Holmes, he will know what to do.'

Chapter 4

A sharp ringing from the telephone woke the dreaming detectives. Lestrade blindly reached for the phone asking abruptly who it was. A second later he ejected out of his chair and shouted, "What the blazes?" Looking at Holmes he shouted "Moriarty has escaped! He left Styles in that damn black Roller and my men lost him!"

Holmes shrugged his shoulders and calmly said, "He won't go far, as he likes to watch whatever he has planned for us."

They were all startled by Harry Houdini standing in the bedroom doorway. His face was washed clean, his hair was neatly combed. He also looked dapper in one of Doctor Watson's best walking suits. Watson looked aghast, 'Why the hide of him! Without even asking,' he thought. Houdini was an athletic man and loved to be well groomed. Watson realised with chagrin, that he never looked this good in this suit.

Holmes was delighted that his old friend was back to his healthy self. "We are about to leave for Styles Manor House. You are welcome to come with us, though first I want you to tell me all that you know about the House."

"Well, I awoke in the dungeons of that dreaded house.

They had me chained in a large room and I can tell you this was their planning room."

Lestrade asked "What you mean planning room."

"On a long table they had a scale model of London showing the main roads and major buildings."

"Tell me more," asked Holmes, as the other detectives all listened intensely.

"The main parts of London were all marked in red."

"Do you remember what these main parts were?" asked Holmes.

A sad and resigned look came over Houdini's face. "There was Number 10 Downing Street, the Houses of Parliament, Scotland Yard and Buckingham Palace, to name a few". Lestrade made a grumbling noise and Houdini continued, "London Bridge and this very house we are all now in."

Holmes gave a dry smile and quipped, "It's amusing that Moriarty ranks me so highly."

Houdini continued, "There was also a blackboard with drawings showing the technical design details of highly explosive bombs."

Lestrade interjected, "That's it! We are moving in right now."

"Not yet," replied Holmes, "Calm down. I want to know more. How did you find your way out of the house, Harry?"

"By some miracle I found a torch in the room and followed its beam through the darkness. There were endless passageways that led nowhere, then like I said, by some miracle I found the right passage that led me to freedom, but unfortunately, I didn't find my darling Bess on the way. She must be so frightened by now."

Lestrade replied, "That's true Holmes, the night Moriarty alias Blinkhorn disappeared through that secret passageway, I told my men to stop searching for it was too dangerous."

Holmes looked in to Lestrade's eyes in disbelief, "You fool," he cried, "if you would have searched, then we wouldn't be in the mess we are in now." Lestrade looked like a little schoolboy that had been scolded. Holmes immediately felt sorry for him and regretted his outburst, "Don't worry," he said patting him on the shoulder, "I'm sorry I yelled at you. We will catch these fiends and bring them all to justice, hopefully to the gallows."

A smile came over Lestrade's face. All the other detectives were now standing with looks of determination on their faces. They wanted to put end to these monsters who threatened their England and possibly the World.

Holmes strode over to his desk. Pulling out its bottom drawer he took out a large ball of string. They all wondered what in blazes was he up to? All except Miss Marple, she gave a little smile and knowingly nodded her head.

Holmes looking at Lestrade demanding, "Now before we go into Styles. I want the whole property surrounded. We don't know just how many secret passageways lead out of this

house. I want your men to cover every inch, and I mean every inch of the perimeter of the Manor House."

Lestrade nodded. "Yes, Mister Holmes, my men are ready to move on your orders." he responded with a quivering voice.

Turning to Houdini, Holmes asked, "Now Harry, do you remember the exact entry point of the yard where your escape tunnel led you to freedom?"

"Well," he said, running his palm through his thick wavey hair, "like I said, the drugs they put into me made everything a little hazy. The only thing I clearly remember is an angel looking down at me with water running from her hands."

Miss Marple rolled her eyes while Bulldog Drummond scoffed, "They must have been good drugs they gave you, Harry." They all laughed and even Holmes gave a little grin.

"Non, my friends he is correct, for at the rear of the house there is a water fountain with the statue of an angel standing in the middle," said a smiling Hercules Poirot. Holmes looked at Lestrade giving him a firm nod. Lestrade gave a knowing look back. He knew this part of the yard would have to be heavily guarded.

The great detectives all knew that this case was the most important of their careers. So many lives depended on them stopping these fiends. Holmes was up against his arch nemesis, Professor Moriarty. Two men hated and despised the other, even though they still had a high respect for their opponent.

Hercules Poirot was going back to a house that still brought him fear from many years ago. He also knew this house would be his doom. Still, he must go for so much depended on his compatriots in this room.

Miss Marple's, Bulldog Drummond's and Jules Margret's sense of personal duty commanded their involvement.

Doctor Watson was always at Holmes side going back to his first case, 'A Study in Scarlet'. He would never forget their most frighting case, 'The Hound of the Baskervilles'. Now this new case may supersede them all. He knows though, whatever happens, he will be standing firmly beside his good friend. With his trusty revolver, he would take on these demons that threaten the free world.

For Inspector Lestrade, it's his job, although he loves to test his wits against the combined wit of these great men.

Then we have poor Harry Houdini, whose beloved wife is at the mercy of these merciless villains. Harry is no ordinary man. He demonstrated his skills by escaping from their clutches. Despite not knowing if his wife Bess is still alive, Harry and his friends won't stop until she is found and the Professor and his associates are behind bars, convicted of their guilt, then taken to the gallows in punishment for their terrible crimes.

They all stood, staring at each other with determined faces. Miss Marple was studying all their faces ever so carefully and she knew it was time to make their move on Styles Manor

House. Holmes looked at Lestrade and he knew what Holmes wanted.

"Yes, gentlemen," he announced, "the Police Bus will be here soon to take us all to Styles Manor House. I not only have the house surrounded, I also have all the surrounding streets heavily guarded. There is no way out. We have them trapped in this nightmare of a house."

"Let us just hope we are not walking into a trap ourselves," answered Holmes. The room fell silent then they were all startled by the blast of a loud horn. Holmes looked down from his window onto Baker Street said, "Well gentlemen, our bus is here. Our business is at hand."

Chapter 5

Visibility in Baker Street was eerily murky, as a heavy blanket of fog oozed up from the depths of the Thames, covering all of London. Misty tendrils surrounded the intrepid detectives as they left Sherlock Holmes's premises, all contributing to their general feeling of unease. They all climbed aboard Scotland Yard's impressive new omnibus. Lestrade was very proud of this latest innovation that promoted the strength of "his" Police Force. "Take a seat Miss Marple and gentlemen. Mister Holmes and Doctor Watson can sit up front with me," he invited. Sitting down Lestrade continued talking about his new vehicle. "This is no ordinary machine," he proudly boasted, but before he could say another word he was interrupted by Jules Maigret.

"Oui, we have had one at my headquarters in Paris for the last six months," he scoffed. "These windows are all bullet proof." With a smile he tapped the bowl of his pipe on the window beside him. "Also, le bus could withstand the explosion of a small bomb. These vehicles are the equivalent of a small tank."

The look on Lestrade's face would curdle Cornish cream! 'How dare you,' he thought. 'Bloody foreign braggart. This is not Paris! How can a people who eat those horrible snails have

the latest in technology, like us British?'

Holmes answered with a smile, "Let's just hope Moriarty does not have one of those large bombs planted for us. That would give this tank-like bus a shake or two, I shudder to think."

All the detectives looked at each other. The look of solemnity on their faces said it all. Could this be their farewell case? Their expressions were all serious, stoical, apart from Miss Marple's. Her gentle expression never changed as her knitting needles continued to work away – knit 3, purl 2, slip 1, pass slip stitch over, repeat, repeat, repeat….

They were all startled by a heavy knock on the omnibus door. The driver pressed the lever and the door edged open. A large burley policeman put his head inside the bus. With a stern voice he said to Inspector Lestrade, "We have police cars in front and behind you, sir. It's going to be a very slow trip to Styles in this fog, mark my words. It's a real pea souper, sir, and not likely to get any better, mark my words."

Lestrade just nodded and waved as the officer left and entered the leading car. The vehicles all proceeded slowly through the encircling fog. Their lights reflecting yellow on the misty shrouds around them. Miss Marple said, "Isn't this so exciting, with the fog and all, I mean?"

Bulldog Drummond gave her a fond, little smile. "It reminds me of a case I had a few years ago," he replied. "It was up in Scotland and the fog was just like this and very exciting too, but our inability to see what surrounded us contributed to our nerves, I must say."

"Well, you survived that one," she said with a smile.

There was no smile on Poirot's face as he could not drag his thoughts from imagining what they would probably encounter at Styles Manor House. This atmosphere was nothing new to him, for Styles was always surrounded by strange, mysterious things.

Maigret was thinking of his beloved Paris. He just wanted this case to be over so he could return home to his apartment and his adored wife. He also knew about these heavy fogs, for in his own country, this is where evil would inevitably lurk.

For Holmes and Watson this was also nothing new for them. They had solved some of their most famous cases in fog, like the one in Baskerville, so similar to this. Holmes seemed to thrive in this atmosphere, just like the criminals he pursued.

Harry Houdini performed most of his magic tricks in complete darkness. This swirling nightmare of fog meant nothing to him. All that was on his mind was the love of his life, Bess. 'Please God, let her still be alive. Oh Lord, please help us to save her.'

Holmes had confirmed to him, "Bess is just a pawn in Moriarty's game. She will be well hidden inside the walls of that house. He is playing cat and mouse with us, for he wants bigger fish to fry than your wife, for you see Harry, he wants me."

The omnibus followed the police cars slowly through the fog. This would be to their advantage as the monsters would not know when they entered the house. Moriarty would be watching close by, but he will not be able to warn them as the telephone lines had been cut and the electricity had been turned off. The only light would come from oil lamps candles and torches. Holmes muttered under his breath, "We will be in the same boat, so let's hope the element of surprise will do it for us."

Harry knew Holmes was a man of his word and he also knew he would not stop till Bess was free.

Watson checked that his revolver was fully loaded which he knew it wasn't. Watson was ex-army and although he was a doctor, he had seen his share of bloody action in India. He was up for a good battle against these fiends who threaten his beloved England. His years in the military had drummed the maxim into him 'to always leave the first chamber of your weapon empty for safety reasons when you are about to go into action. You don't fully load until you are there.' Watson took a bullet from his vest pocket and placed it into the empty chamber. He was now fully ready for anything that Styles and Moriarty would throw up at him.

Lestrade sat up the front next to the omnibus driver, sitting ramrod straight, shoulders back with his chest proudly pronounced. In his eyes this was his show and it really was, although he had the world's most famous detectives at his side. Still though it would be Sherlock Holmes who called all the moves. Life is full of disappointments.

The sound of Big Ben rang through the streets of London as the omnibus and its entourage slowly left the city.

In just over an hour the police omnibus and its occupants silently parked outside the gates of Styles Manor House.

Chapter 6

Hidden inside the bus the detectives' eyes were busily investigating the layout of Styles Manor House and the surrounding overgrown grounds. The towering trees and dense bushes made it difficult to anticipate where danger lurked. Peering through the iron gates the swirling fog made the house look very sinister, indeed. At least it appeared as if Lestrade's men were well hidden (if they were there at all), for not a soul, nor a Bobbie's hat or clodhopper boots could be seen. Lestrade had a worried look on his face, "Where are my men?" he whispered to himself.

The great detectives could not be blamed for thinking they had driven into one of Moriarty's planned traps. "Thank God the bus is bomb proof," said Watson, "Supposedly!" Still, no one felt safe. The only sound outside was the wind blowing through the trees. They were all startled by a light tap on the bus door. Lestrade was relieved to be looking at the face of one of his senior men. He opened the door, asking "What's happening? Is all is going to plan."

The Sergeant answered, "We are ready to move on the house at your command, sir."

Holmes bluntly interjected, "Make sure you have the back of the house well covered, especially around that fountain."

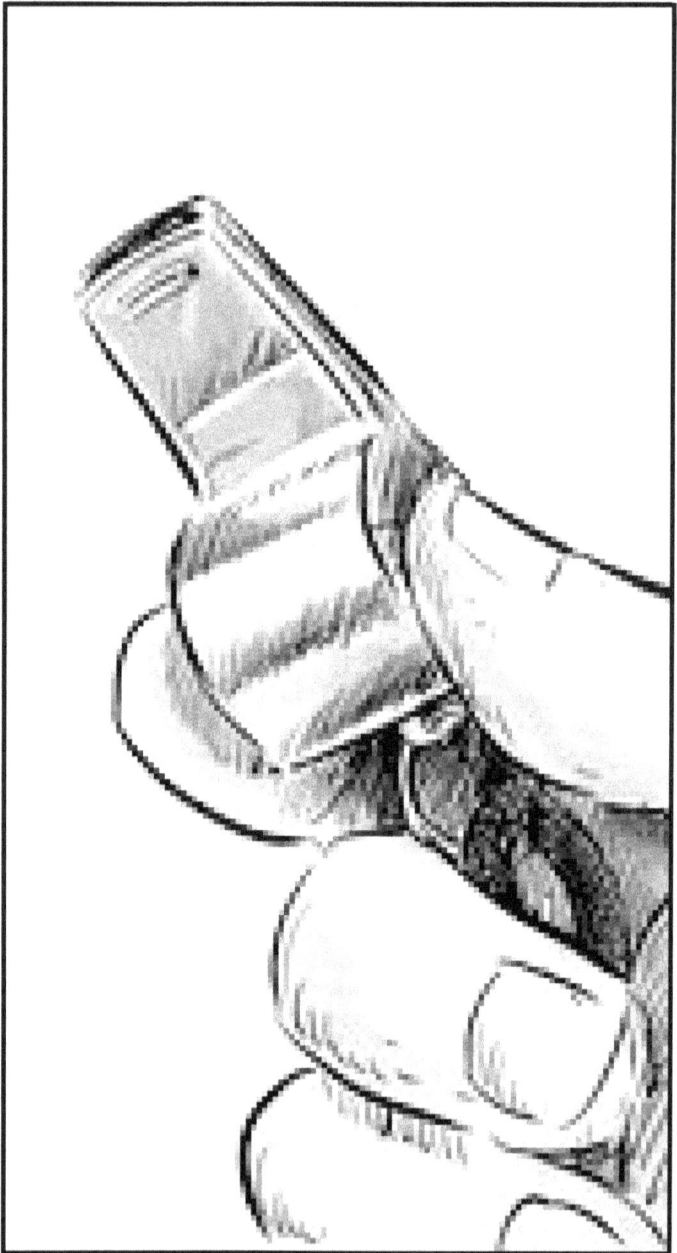

"We have Mr Holmes," the officer answered, "we have followed your orders to the letter."

Lestrade's face was aghast at the temerity of Holmes daring to take charge of his operation, although he realised that Holmes knew what he was doing. A large basket full of new-fangled battery operated torches had been packed onto the seat beside Lestrade and he handed each detective one as they stepped from the bus. Delightedly now that things were finally underway, he said, "As we are luckily under the cover of this fog, we will hit the house." He held a shiny whistle up for all to see, "When I blow this three times, simultaneously, we are going in through the front and back doors. My men are all ready to move when I do this." Holmes nodded his approval, and a proud smile came over Lestrade's face, "Well let's do it!" he cried. With that he blew the whistle, the peep, peep, peeps echoing through the darkness.

The burly officers pounded both the front and back doors down with a resulting clatter and they all charged into the house, yelling loudly to add to the resulting confusion. Turning their torches on they scoured the whole house. After spreading out to cover all of the floors the detectives again met in the entrance hall, shaking their heads. They stared at each other in disbelief because the house seemed to be empty. How on earth?

Holmes told Lestrade to have the power turned back on so they could continue to search in a better light. At that moment the sound of heavy gunfire came from the back of the house. "They are escaping through the secret passageway," shouted Lestrade.

"Hold your positions men!" shouted Holmes.

Shortly, the gunfire stopped, and an officer ran through the doorway. "Inspector Lestrade," he gasped, "we have captured eight men who were trying to escape. They came out through that stone fountain that Mr Holmes told us about!"

Holmes asked, "Were any of them women?"

"No," the officer answered.

"Well, one man and two women are still in this house," replied Holmes.

Lestrade looked deeply puzzled, "How do you come to that number?" he asked.

"Remember, Harry said that he heard twelve voices. Well, we know that Moriarty escaped so that leaves 3 more that are in this house." At that moment all the lights came on. The house looked very different now, in the style of a grand English country residence, that had given it its name, Styles Manor House.

Pondering for a moment, Hercule Poirot announced, "They are in the walls. There are tunnels, n'est pas?"

"Yes," cried Harry, "they have my Bess in there with them."

Holmes said, "It will be safer if just Harry and I go inside the walls for he has been in there and knows the layout."

Looking at Lestrade he added, "I want you to put two men on every door in this house, and another 4 on the fountain in case they try to trick us and double back. No one is leaving here."

Lestrade just nodded in agreement. They all went into the dining room where this adventure had originally started. There was the dining table where they all sat, awaiting the events that were to unfold, however no one could have anticipated this. Holmes' eyes searched the room for Moriarty. He secretly believed that somehow, someway, he would be in this house. For Moriarty loved to observe his plans come to fruition and Holmes believed that they were all in mortal danger. Moriarty wanted them all in this house, his plan would be to trap them all and finally dispose of them.

Going over to the secret panel in the fireplace, Holmes opened it. Putting his hand in his pocket, Holmes took out his ever present ball of string. Giving Harry some string, he told him to lead the way. Once the panel's door had been shut, the passageways were in complete darkness. Turning on their torches, they followed the beams shining across the dusty floor. Occasionally there was another hallway leading somewhere else. "Goodness, Harry," whispered Holmes, "how did you ever find your way out of this maze?"

"It took me a while but then I saw the clues, Sherlock."

"What did you see?"

Harry pointed to the dusty floor, "I found an area where there was no dust on the floors or walls, for this was the area they were using all the time."

Holmes smiled, "You would make a great detective Harry, should you decide to change your profession."

"No, I will leave that to you, Sherlock." They continued with their search, it seemed to take forever.

Back in the dining room Watson was deeply worried, 'Why hadn't Holmes taken him into those catacombs hidden inside these walls?' Lestrade and all the great detectives had worried looks on their faces too. Holmes and Houdini had been gone for a long time. Holmes had taken Lestrade's whistle and told him he would blow it if they needed help.

Harry whispered, "Look there, Sherlock!" On the floor in front of them was no dust "This is it!" Tip toeing a short way down the passageway they were met by a closed door. Holmes turned the doorknob and threw the door open. Shining their touches around the room they were shocked to find it empty again.

Finally following the string line back to the dining room, they let the others know of their failure to find anyone, especially Bess. Houdini despondently sat at the table with his hands over his face, "What have they done to my Bess?"

Lestrade shouted, "How could they escape?"

The all watched Holmes as he walked over to the two policemen guarding the door. They were both very tall men with broad shoulders. Holmes looked one of them straight in the face and said, "How are you today, Mr Moriarty?"

Chapter 7

Everyone looked startled on hearing Moriarty's name. Lestrade shouted "What the blazes?" and shouted, "Seize him!" to his men. Before Moriarty could even blink once, four burly officers grabbed hold of him. "Now you two men, cuff each arm then cuff the other manacle to your own arm. He isn't going anywhere."

Holmes nodded in agreement, "Bring him over to the table and we will all sit down," he added.

His nostrils flaring like a wild bull, and with steam coming out of his ears, Houdini headed straight for Moriarty. "Where is my Bess," he cried, "I'll kill you if you don't tell me. I'll kill you three times over." Two other officers grabbed him before he could reach their perpetual nemesis. His anger combined with his brutal strength, so they struggled to hold him off.

Holmes patted him kindly on the shoulder, "Now sit down and behave yourself. This is not helping us to find Bess," he calmly said.

The great detectives all sat in the same seats as they had on that fateful night, the precursor to these strange events that had led them here. The officers pushed Moriarty onto a chair, to the left of Holmes. Lestrade sat on Holme's right,

repeatedly craning around Holmes to keep an eye on Moriarty. No one said a word. They were all studying the evil creature before them. Even though Moriarty was internationally infamous, for a number of the detectives, this was actually the first time they had actually laid eyes on him. Up till then, he had been a demonic creature of mystery.

Holmes looked at the box on the table in front of him. The magic box from that fateful night. Holmes whispered, "This Jack-in-the-box of yours was a great little trick. Even the puzzle you contrived with the number plate on your car," he snapped his fingers. "You like to play silly little games with silly little clues." Ignoring the taunts, Moriarty's face never changed, his cold black eyes just stared at the great detectives sitting around the table.

Their eyes were studying him as well. Hercule Poirot could not believe how evil this man looked. He looked like the devil incarnate. Moriarty deserved to stay in the walls of this monstrous house for ever. If only they could imprison him here and be reassured that he could never escape. All Poirot wanted was to be out of this place and back home in his ordered apartment.

Miss Marple loved to study people's faces, and in her lifetime, she had met many normal looking people without a shred of compassion who were able to kill and main without compunction. This face, his face, however, her terrified. The eyes invited you to your death. She remembered the night he disappeared, in this very room, how did he do it? Obviously, he has the ability to disappear, just like Houdini himself. She looked over at Houdini and gave him a gentle smile. He didn't smile back at her. He was wearing a look that could kill.

Bulldog Drummond had dealt with some of the most hardened criminals the world had known, but this Moriarty was someone very strange. No, more than strange. He was almost inhuman. Even though he was manacled to two officers, it still didn't feel safe to be in this room with him.

Jules Maigret, he too had met evil many times before, though this time he believed that he had never seen anything just so evil. He looked down the length of his tobaccoless pipe, daring to stare into Moriarty's dark, lifeless eyes. He steeled himself to prevent a shudder from showing in his expression.

Houdini glared into those dark cold eyes, but his eyes were just as dark and cold. But his were not lifeless. They burned with rage. He didn't fear Moriarty so much as he wanted to kill him for taking Bess. The two officers were still sitting at Moriarty's side, to prevent him just in case he tried to get to his prey.

None of this scrutiny seemed to worry Moriarty. His face never changed; his eyes never blinked. Doctor Watson was one of the rare few who had ever seen the real, unmasked Professor Moriarty, and had survived the experience. He would never forget the time when he almost killed his dear friend, Sherlock Holmes. How close he had come!

Tapping the box once again, Holmes said, "I know you still have two women and a man remaining in this house. I am sick of your false clues, the little games that you play. What do you call them Poirot?" he asked,

"Oh yes, the red herrings," Poirot answered. "They are of course the false clues meant to distract one from the real crime and the real villain. Back in the seventeenth century people were outraged about high society having these barbaric fox hunts. Foxes hunted to their death by packs of vicious dogs. To prevent attacks people would smoke the herrings till they turned a reddish colour. They would then tie the herrings with ropes and drag them through woods and fields so the pungent odor would cover the scent of the fox, confusing the dogs."

"Ah yes," cried Holmes, looking straight into Moriarty's eyes, "and that's exactly what we have here."

Moriarty slowly blinked his eyes for the first time and his face became enraged. "Blast you Holmes, you may have me, but we will all die together." Looking at the mahogany, long case, grandfather clock near the fireplace he shouted, "Time is almost up."

It was ten to ten, everyone started to panic apart from Doctor Watson. Pointing to the crossed swords hanging over the fireplace, he states, "Doesn't that look like they are making an "X"?"

Holmes jumping from his chair, exclaimed, "My dear

Watson, you are a genius!"

Watson blushed and his face went a bright red colour. Lestrade grumbled under his breath, "He's far from that," which no one heard for they were all looking at the crossed swords.

Holmes cried, "Look that is the "X", now just look at the floor! See the yellow rug that is the "Y" now! See the little zebras on the rug." Holmes looked at Moriarty, "There is your "XYZ".

Moriarty laughed scornfully, "You are too late Holmes. Time is about up!"

Poirot slapped his forehead. "Sacre bleu, where are my little grey cells? Under this floor is one of best wine cellars in all of England."

Quickly they rolled back the rug and saw a large trap door that had been completely covered by the carpet. Pulling it open, they saw a steep, wooden staircase leading down into darkness. Following the beam of his torch, Holmes led them down into the cellar. There were rows upon rows of tall shelves filled with bottles of wine and wooden wine barrels, all in a row. The room was large, and the rows of shelves stretched into the darkened distance. Then, at the end of the next row, they saw them. Right at the back of the room up against the wall gathered the three elusive assailants they had been searching for.

Sitting on a chair in front of them sat a relieved looking,

Bess Houdini. Harry started to move forward. One of the ladies shouted, "Don't move!" She was holding a German Lugar to Bess's head. Holmes was looking at the contraption sitting on the table beside them. It was a time bomb. There were only fifteen seconds left until it exploded, and they would all be killed. He shouted, "Drop your weapons right now," and amazingly they did. Lestrade rushed forward to gather up the guns. Holmes ordered, "Watson, break open the lid on that barrel of red wine beside you."

Watson picked up a wooden mallet and with one big hit, broke open the lid on the barrel. In one swift motion Holmes picked up the time bomb and dropped it into the barrel of red wine.

They all waited to be blown to pieces, They waited and waited, and nothing happened. Their grim faces slowly relaxed to smiles. Houdini ran to Bess and untied her, kissed and hugged her tightly. They were all now safe now, thanks to Sherlock Holmes.

Lestrade sputtered, "How the hell did you know that would work?"

"I didn't, I just hope the acid in the red wine would do something to the timing in the bomb which it did."

"Blimey you are a cool one, Mr Holmes," he added, "now let's get upstairs and take care of Mr Moriarty."

Back up in the room Moriarty was still sitting in his chair with the two officers beside him. Looking at Holmes he growled, "You may have won this time, Holmes. But take my word for it, no cell will ever hold me."

"Oh yes it will," responded Lestrade, "I'll have you down in my deepest cell and there will be guards watching you day and night. That will take care of the likes of you!"

Chapter 8

Not long out of their respective beds after a mutually restless night, Holmes and Watson sat in their wing-back chairs in front of the blazing fireplace in the study. The morning had a very icy chill, although these two gentlemen were quite warm. Miss Hudson had just delivered a pot of tea and buttered toast, generously topped with plum jam. Watson was reading this morning's London Times while devouring his toast and jam. Holmes had just filled his pipe from the Persian slipper and stared into the burning fireplace while his mind traversed idly over their last case. There was something worrying Holmes about this very strange affair.

Watson laughed abruptly at an article he was reading, "Our good friend, Inspector Lestrade has taken all the credit for solving and capturing that fiend, Professor Moriarty. I quote, with the help of Mister Sherlock Holmes and aided by some of the world's greatest detectives, my wonderful London Bobbies and I have foiled and captured that evil criminal, Professor Moriarty. He foolishly tried to outwit Scotland Yard and he failed. There is a photo of Inspector Lestrade, beaming, on the front page of The Times. Why the hide of this nincompoop!" scoffed Watson.

Holmes just smiled, "Tut, tut, Watson, we all work together in our little ways." he replied.

Watson harrumphed and then helped himself to some more toast with jam. Reading further he almost choked, "Listen to this Holmes," he cried. On the very next page was a photo of Harry Houdini. Watson read out aloud, "Harry Houdini will be performing this Saturday night at London's Palladium Theater. See with your own eyes if he can escape from the Egyptian Pharaoh's Tomb of Death. He will be locked into this Tomb of Death, not by one great detective, there will be seven great detectives present. They will make sure there is no way of escaping. One of the great detectives will be Mister Sherlock Holmes himself. Also, Inspector Lestrade from Scotland Yard will be there." Watson laughed once more.

Holmes stood up dressed in his favorite long, maroon, quilted dressing gown. He walked over to the window and looked down onto Baker Street. It was quite busy for this time of morning. People hurrying about up and down the footpaths. Cars and buses are going back and forth, intent on their usual pursuits. 'Ah yes, it's Saturday morning, that's why it's so busy. My mind has been on other things.' he thought. Then for a second, he glimpsed it. There was a man standing in the doorway across the street looking up at him. He stepped back quickly into the shadows of the doorway. Holmes knew the man was still hiding in those shadows. Looking over his pipe Holmes exhaled his pipe's smoke, obscuring the window. He too was now partially hidden. It had only taken a second, but he knew his assailant would now know that he was on to him. Holmes was sure the man had disappeared through the shop door, and he would more than likely disappeared out through the back door as well.

Holmes noticed a black taxi pull up at their front door and smiled as he watched Harry and Bess Houdini step out of the cab. Holmes walked over and sat down in his chair not saying a word, waiting while Houdini paid the taxi fare. While he was waiting, he thought about who had been spying on them. He knew they had numerous enemies, and not just Moriarty, though Moriarty would not leave his mind. Finally, there was a knock at the door and Miss Hudson showed the Houdinis in. Holmes and Watson jumped up to greet them. Smiling, they all hugged.

Bess could not stop thanking them for saving her. Harry nodded in agreement. "Mister Holmes," she went on, "you have the greatest mind not just in criminology, your mind is full of knowledge on many subjects."

Holmes blushed, "You are so kind," he exclaimed, "though it's all in a day's work." They all laughed at his modesty.

Noticing The Times that Watson had casually tossed onto the coffee table when they entered, Harry raised up his hand and said, "I see you have been reading about my show at the London Palladium Theater. It is true. I want you and the other detectives to be there on the night. This is going to be my greatest ever show. The Royal Family will be there in their Royal Box looking down at me. It is going to be a black-tie affair, so I want you all dressed in a top hat and tails. This will be a night of nights! The who's who of London will all be there." Bess had a worried look on her face.

"What is troubling you?" Holmes asked.

Bess slowly spoke, "You see Mister Holmes, this Egyptian Death Box is a large mummy's coffin and anyone who has gone into it before has mysteriously died. They say an Egyptian Pharaoh once occupied it." They all raised their eyes in amazement. "Well," Bess continued, "his ghost or spirit will not let them leave. Five men have died inside this Pharaoh's coffin."

All eyes stared at Harry in disbelief. "Well, you all know me," he shrugged. "Once I heard these stories, I just had to have it as I thought that it would be a marvelous accompaniment to my act. I traveled to Egypt and paid a fortune to obtain it. I, myself, do not believe these stories though the publicity will make me a fortune."

"Yes," Bess shouted angrily, "and it could make me a widow. Did you ever stop to think of that Mr Houdini?"

Harry put his arms around her. "Don't worry I'll have Sherlock and Doctor Watson plus all the other great detectives there to watch over me."

She shook her head, "I can never win with this man. He

is too smart for his own good."

Doctor Watson added, "Those Egyptians are a mysterious lot. They are still finding hidden tombs containing corpses who apparently died from strange curses. I would stay right away from it all. I am a doctor, and that stuff is beyond me. I am not embarrassed to confess that it scares me."

"Yes," Bess cried, "that's what I have been trying to tell him."

Harry was getting angry at his beloved wife's fears. "I understand what you are saying, however I have checked the coffin or death camber as I like to call it." Bess rolled her eyes. "I have thoroughly scoured every inch, inside and out. Lid and coffin. I have been all over it and it's very safe. There is no way I am going to change my mind, so that is my final word." To change the subject, he looked over at Holmes, he asked "What you are thinking about Sherlock?"

Holmes was still looking out the window where he again saw the dark figure of a man standing in the doorway across the street. "There is a lot more to worry about than your magic show, I am afraid to say."

Before he could say another word, the door flew open and standing there was Inspector Lestrade. He was frothing at the mouth and shouting, "Gor blimey, Moriarty has escaped."

On hearing this name Bess Houdini screamed and fainted. As she fell Harry luckily caught her before she hit the floor. "Quick!", shouted Holmes, "Lie her on the sofa. Watson pour a cup of tea!" Watson poured the freshly made hot tea from the tea pot into a Royal Dolton cup and handed it to Holmes. Kneeling beside her Holmes softly whispered "You are safe. I'll never let him harm you."

Her eyes fluttered open, "That man is so evil", she cried.

Holmes calmly replied, "Now sip some tea Mrs Houdini. Inspector Lestrade will have two of his London Bobbies watching you day and night."

She smiled at Holmes and looked up at Inspector Lestrade, who nodded to her in agreement. Bess looked over at the doorway where two burly Bobbies stood. She felt a lot safer as she sipped her tea. "Thank you, Mr Holmes. I know, you will catch this horrible man."

Houdini angrily spoke to Lestrade, "How in blazes did he escape from your escape proof cell?"

"Well, he didn't just escape through one door, he vanished through four doors. When I say he vanished that's just what he did. Just like you do Mr Houdini, he vanished straight through the iron bars."

"That's it," cried Houdini in mortification, "Moriarty did discover my tricks. When they drugged me, I believed that I had fooled them, but this Moriarty is so cunning."

Lestrade slowly rubbed his jaw. "Now what just are theses tricks if I may ask?"

Harry looked over at Bess lying on the sofa, "Only the ones close to me know my secrcts."

Bess nodded, "Tell them, Harry," she whispered.

All eyes were fixed on Harry Houdini's face. The whole world would love to know his secrets and these men in this room were about to find out. Holmes blew out some smoke from his pipe as even he was puzzled by Harry's legendary escapology powers. Harry took a key from his vest pocket. Holding it up for all to see he admitted, shrugging, "I have taught myself to be able to swallow it and bring it back up into my mouth on demand." Lestrade face took on a horrified expression as Harry swallowed the key. He could still talk normally as he walked around the room. "You see Inspector Lestrade, your London Police Force all use the same key for all of your locks. If you have one key, you can open all of them."

"Blimey", shouted Lestrade, "that's how he has done it!"

Harry made a gurgling sound and the next second the key had been regurgitated back in Harry's hand. They were all astonished, even Doctor Watson "I have never seen anything like it before." he claimed.

Lestrade added, "We have no idea where Moriarty is. No clues at all. He has vanished."

Holmes called Lestrade over to the window. After telling him about the man he had seen in the opposite doorway, Lestrade asked, "Do you think it could be him?"

"I believe it is him," answered Holmes, "it's the way Moriarty plays the game. Now send the two Bobbies down there to investigate. He himself will not be there. Have them thoroughly search the property upstairs and down. All the rooms, hallways, window ledges, cupboards and the basement. Don't miss anything or anywhere that someone could hide or leave a clue. Tell them to ask a lot of questions of the people living in the building." Doctor Watson and Lestrade were shocked to hear this request for usually Holmes would always do this investigative work himself, not trusting anyone else to spot the nuances essential to his thought patterns. "We will wait here for their discoveries, so make yourself at home", he gestured.

Houdini replied, "I must notify my people to cancel the show for Saturday night."

Holmes said bluntly, "No, the show goes ahead." They all looked at him strangely. "For this is where we will set a trap to catch Moriarty. It's been his plan all along to have us all there for his final act. He wants not just to outshine the great Houdini but also to shame the World's Greatest Detectives."

Bess cried, "Oh no. You will all be in such danger."

"Don't worry", assured Holmes, "Lestrade will have his men all over the place inside and out. They will be disguised so Inspector Lestrade and I will be the only ones who know who they are." Lestrade razed his eyebrows but ruefully nodded yes. "Like I said, I will not let anyone harm you."

At that moment the Bobbies entered the room. One of them was holding a note pad, "Ah good," cried Holmes, "you have taken notes. Tell what you have found out."

"Well sir", answered the Bobbie, "you were right Mr Holmes, the man was gone. People living in the building told us that a strange man had been living there for six months and he fitted the description you gave us."

"What the blazes", shouted Lestrade, "you mean to say he has been watching our every move all this time?"

"Yes, sir", added the Officer. "In his room, we discovered a telescope set up at the window aimed at this very room."

"Blimy, he has been playing cat and mouse with us all this time", scolded Lestrade.

"Like I said", Holmes replied, "he has planned this like one big game. Harry's show on Saturday night is the grand finale. He used those Germans in the basements at Styles for his own ploy, and they will still be a worry in the future. We are the ones he is really after and I am top of his list. He has been living across the street from me all this time. Watching. Waiting. Planning. Making the perfect plan like you say, Lestrade, playing the cat and mouse. He likes to play the long game where many suffer, even the little people that aren't really in the game. We will have to all be ready for Saturday night, for he has been planning this for a long time.

"Lestrade you will have to pick your best men to go undercover as they have to play their parts to perfection. No mishaps or it will all come undone."

"I have the men that will pull this off. I have all the faith in my men."

Holmes said, "Theses two men of yours here will be great for the night as well."

The two Bobbies had big smiles on their faces "They are two of my best men, always by my side" acknowledged Lestrade.

Holmes nodded to them in admiration, "It's going to be a very dangerous night. Keep your wits about you. Be alert. Question every odd thing." Both men nodded to Holmes, all of the London Bobbies admired Mr Sherlock Holmes, despite Inspector Lestrade always being very jealous of Holme's successes and believing himself to be above Holmes. It never bothered him to take the credit for Holmes' detective work. Despite this, the London constabulary idolized Sherlock Holmes, and these men were thrilled to be working with him and vowed to do their best.

"Well let's start moving as we have a lot of work to do before Saturday night", ordered Lestrade.

"Yes, I agree", answered Holmes, "the game is afoot."

Chapter 9

Holmes and Lestrade were shocked at the look on Houdini's face. He walked over to the window staring with a face of blankness.

Lestrade asked, "What in blazes is wrong with him?"

He turned and nodded for them to come over. His face was full of pain and torment.

"What is troubling you?" asked Holmes.

He looked at his wife, Bess who was being comforted by Doctor Watson. She was looking up at the two tall Bobbies with admiration and feeling safe.

"You see gentlemen I lied to you, for I have met this Moriarty before."

"What in blazes!" cried Lestrade.

Holmes held up his hand for him to stop,

"Continue." asked Holmes.

"Six months ago, I was working in my factory in New York. I was working on a new escape box for my show. In walked Moriarty with two of his henchmen and very mean they looked too! He told me immediately, if I did not do what I was told something terrible would happen to Bess! My temper exploded, even though I had no chance against these two gorillas. They just threw me to the floor. They needed me to teach them how I do my lock tricks and safe cracking powers. They knew I was

going to London in six months time, and if I said one word to anyone, they would know, as they had people everywhere."

Lestrade raised his eyes wide open on hearing about the safe cracking.

"That's how they did it!" he bellowed.

Houdini looked Lestrade hard in the face. "Once, in London, they tried to contact me and I would not take their calls. So, I hired a couple of private detectives to watch over us, especially Bess. One night, the two detectives vanished... disappeared and were never found. Bess and I were taken hostage and you know the rest. I blame myself for what has happened. If only I had come to you Sherlock, you would have known what to do."

Lestrade did not look happy, "What about Scotland Yard?"

Harry nodded with a bowed head, "You are right," he whispered.

Holmes patted him on the shoulder, "We are dealing with one of the smartest and deadliest criminals of all time. Harry, you, and Bess are so incredibly lucky that you survived and trust me, I will bring this monster to justice, with the help of Inspector Lestrade of course."

A big smile came over Lestrade's face. Watson and Bess could not hear what they were talking about though. Watson grunted, knowing Lestrade would take all the credit for himself.

In Watson's eyes Lestrade was a fool and Lestrade believed the same about Watson. Holmes never looked for any awards or admirations. He loved his work, and the powers of his criminal deductions were admired all around the world. Holmes liked nothing more than to bring evil criminals to justice and Moriarty was the evillest, criminal of all time.

Lestrade, giving his best Scotland yard face, looked Houdini straight in his dark-brown eyes. "Now, Mister Houdini, are you sure there is nothing else you are not telling us?"

Bess asked Watson, "What are they talking about over there?"

With a smile Watson said, "Do not worry young lady they are planning everything for tomorrow night."

She sipped some more warm tea and wished she were back home in America. She always loved touring the world and being on stage with her husband although now home seemed so far away.

Houdini told Lestrade he had no more to tell. "They drugged me, and I told them nothing. I know now that is not true, they got all my secrets."

Holmes asked, "Did anything happen in New York at your factory that you can remember?"

A strange look came over Houdini's face, "Well… yes, there was something a bit strange."

Lestrade shot back, "And what was that may I ask?"

Holmes smiled, "Tell us my good friend."

"When Moriarty and his two henchmen came into my magic factory Moriarty could not stop looking at my Chamber of Death that had just arrived from Egypt. The story about it had been in the papers all around world. So, he said 'You are the only man in the world game enough to go inside this thing. Before we leave, I want to show you something.' With that he opened the door of the Death Chamber and walked inside."

"Can you tell me more?" asked Holmes.

Houdini laughed, "You amaze me Sherlock. Well, he was in there for a good five minutes."

"Blimey!" cried Lestrade, "He really is a strange one this Moriarty."

Houdini continued, "Yes, even his two gorillas were frightened of this Death Chamber, and they were so happy when he finally came out. It was like he was showing me he was the one to fear and there will be no escaping him. I know this now to be true! Holmes, it's up to you to stop this monster, not for me, but for Bess, we must save her from his clutches."

They all looked over at Bess she looked so innocent sitting on the sofa, sipping her tea.

Lestrade spoke up, "Like I said, I will have these two fine Bobbies watching her day and night." The bobbies looked over at them and smiled. Holmes knew she would be safe in their hands for he believed Moriarty was now working on his own. He had no more henchmen left to help him. He was still dangerous though, even on his own, and it would take all the great detectives to stop and capture him.

Holmes did not want to be using Bess as the bait. But it was the only way to finish Moriarty for the last time. The plan was now in place, the trap was set, and Holmes would finally put an end to this evil person.

There will be so many people at the London Palladium, and this is the only floor. Moriarty like Holmes was a master of disguise and with all those people, there would be many places to hide.

Lestrade said, "Well gentlemen, and lady, it is time to leave. Like I said, Mister Holmes and Doctor Watson, I will pick you up in our police bus tomorrow night."

They all left with best wishes. However, there was still more planning to do.

Chapter 10

Lestrade ordered his two Bobbies to stay with the Houdini's. "Men, I am ordering you to not leave their sides, not even for a moment. Even if you hear or see something suspicious, you will stay put. I will have your guts for garters if you do not obey. You will be relieved later tonight and will be back on watch later tomorrow. The men relieving you will have a password so that you know whom they are and that I have sent them. The password is "MAGIC". Both men nodded at the Inspector in agreement. Bess smiled in relief. She was now feeling safe with these two big men looking after her. Holmes also smiled at her for he knew she would now be secure, and he could redirect his mind from that all-consuming worry and re-commence concentrating on solving the case.

Holmes and Watson wished their visitors goodbye and told them that they would see them on Saturday night at the performance. As he was leaving, Lestrade said he would collect all of the great detectives in his police bus to take them to the London Palladium on Saturday night. Holmes thanked him, saying, "That will be fine. We will all be ready." They all said goodbye to Holmes and Watson who wearily shut and locked their front door, relieved that they were alone again and could concentrate without disruption. Tiredly they climbed the stairs to Holme's study where he poured each of them a generous tot of aged Scotch Whisky. Rather quickly they drank it down, and they each retired to their respective bedrooms to sleep.

Everyone was looking forward to Saturday night. Not only to see Harry's escape trick, but just maybe, to put an end to the infamous career of this horrible creature, Professor Moriarty.

The next morning after a leisurely breakfast of haddock, mushrooms and toast and plentiful cups of strong tea, Holmes and Watson were again in the study, sitting back in their wingback chairs looking into the burning fire once more. "We must stop this terrible man," Holmes whispered. "No one is safe, not even us, till we stop him once and for all."

Watson took out his revolver, "Yes, Holmes and this time I am going to make sure of it. Mister Moriarty will not be going to goal. It's the undertaker then straight to the grave for him." Holmes blew out some smoke from his pipe, nodding in agreement. "Do you think Bess will be safe?" asked Watson.

"I believe she will, Watson, but then like I said, with this devil you never really know what he is thinking or planning. I am sure it's all going to happen on Saturday night at the Palladium. This is what he has planned from the beginning, for all of us. There is no way to escape it. So, we will all have to be on guard. Vigilance is the key."

Watson opened his revolver and re-checked the bullets for the third time. "Oh, I'll be ready, my good friend, you can count on that."

"I know that Watson. I can always count you, my good old Watson." They poured some more tea and contemplated their next move. Or rather, Watson was thinking of what Holmes' next ingenious move would be. Just like a game of chess it goes on until it ends in check mate. Watson quietly chuckled. He knew that Holmes would not want to make a hasty mistake. The room was silent except for the clock ticking on the mantel over the fireplace. The fire was dying down. As it was chilly that morning, Watson put some more logs into the smoldering ashes. It wasn't long before the room was warm once more. Still the silence between the two men continued.

Despite his silence, Watson knew Holmes' mind was working furiously. With each inhalation from his pipe, Holmes' mind delved deeper into his encyclopedic knowledge of crime, and reasoning. You may ask why reasoning? Well, Holmes always surmised there was strong relationship between the reason for a crime and the plot that ultimately develops to successfully commit it. Just like a game of chess, you had to know where each move would take you. Would it lead to falling into someone else's trap or the successful setting of your own trap. In the past Holmes' theory had been well proven resulting in his successful solving of so many cases. The case of the "Hound of the Baskervilles" was a great example. Just like they were in this case, they were up against a very evil mind that only Holmes could master and defeat. Watson knew he could not help because Holmes had to unravel this puzzle by himself. Moriarty and Holmes were playing a game of chess, with checkmate meaning death for one of them.

The woodpile depleted, the logs were still crackling in the fireplace, sending sparks up the chimney into the evening sky. Darkness was slowly creeping through the window absorbing the remaining light. The men had practically sat in silence all day. "It won't be long now, Watson," whispered Holmes.

This quiet comment made Watson feel very uneasy. "What do you mean?" he asked.

"Well," answered Holmes, "in another hour when it's a bit darker, you and I are going to cross over the road to investigate that room ourselves."

"Do you think those Bobbies missed something? asked Watson anxiously, fear tightening his belly.

"No," he smiled, "thought I know Moriarty better than anyone. You and I will search the place from top to bottom. Keep that revolver ready," he quickly added.

"Why? Do you think Moriarty will come back?" asked Watson.

"I am sure of it, my dear Watson. He could even be watching us right now." Watson's simmering fear heightened, and he gulped. "Don't worry my friend, we will play his game very carefully." Holmes said with a knowing smile on his face.

After an hour had passed, Holmes stood up taking off his dressing gown and laying it over the wingback chair. Going over to the coat rack he put on his dark frockcoat and placed his deerstalker hat on his head. "Once again, the game is afoot, Watson we must move swiftly and silently. We must be very vigilant." Watson shrugged into his deep grey overcoat and put on his bowler hat. Now they were dressed for action. Holmes had a small revolver which he always carried, and Watson had his heavy army revolver, that he was never without. Collecting their walking canes from the umbrella stand, another handy weapon to have, they were on their way.

***

The two men crept silently down the stairs, even though they were still inside Holmes' house. Before opening the front door Watson ensured that there were no lights visible in the interior before Holmes slowly opened the front door. Ensuring there was no one hidden across the road, they stealthily emerged. Under the cover of darkness and making sure to avoid the patches of light thrown by the gas street lights, they crossed the road. They stood in front of a well-known bakery, famous for its bread and pies. The business only occupied the lower level. On the top floor were four rented apartments. The front one was the one Moriarty had rented under the name of Blinkhorn.

Ensuring that they were not being observed, or worse, followed, Watson closely shadowed Holmes down the alleyway at the side of the building. Halfway along was a doorway, amazingly it was not locked. Entering, they slowly crept inside, finding themselves in a long hallway, dimly lit with one meager bulb. They climbed a steep staircase, leading them to the upstairs apartments. Holmes took out his small revolver and pointed to the front apartment. Watson reassured himself that his army revolver was still in his coat pocket. After Holmes had used his lock picks to unlock the simple mechanism, he pushed the door open so very gently, shining the torch beam around the room. They were shocked to find no one there. The room was empty. They now had to wait for their visitor to arrive. Watson shone the torch onto another closed door.

Holmes aimed his revolver at the door as Watson flung it open. It was a wardrobe full of clothes. Holmes noticed a suitcase hidden right at the back, under the hanging clothes. Removing it carefully, he took it over and placed it on a table. Watson walked over and peered at the telescope that was aimed out the window, pointing to Holmes' apartment window. Sitting down, he looked through it. "This is amazing, Holmes," he cried, "the blighter was watching our every move!"

Holmes didn't answer, he was too excited by what he had found. It was Moriarty's disguises and Holmes was fascinated by them. Holmes was a master of disguise himself, and now he had his archenemy's little bag of tricks, right in front of him. There was the nose he wore as Blinkhorn and the thick glasses he wore too. This is why Holmes hadn't recognized him. Holmes knew those deadly eyes so well, after staring into them on those high Reichenbach waterfalls where he almost lost his life. He would never forget them.

There were bushy sideburns that the Bobbie had worn at Styles Manor House. Moriarty had made a mistake not wearing glasses with them, or had he made a mistake? This may have been his plan after all, surmised Holmes, for after all, his plan was to escape later, which he actually did.

Then he saw a crumpled newspaper clipping at the bottom of the case. Opening it up, it read, '*Harry Houdini will be performing this Saturday night at the London Palladium. Come along and watch with your own eyes. You still will not believe it is possible! See him escape from the Egyptian Tomb of Death.*'

Engrossed, Holmes and Watson didn't see the dark figure creeping like a ghost from the depths of the closet. Holmes was holding up the newspaper clipping he was reading, and Watson was still looking through the telescope. A thin long blade was thrust down towards Holmes' face. It split the paper he was reading down the middle and missed his face by a hair's breadth. Once more the blade plunged down, but this time Holmes stopped it with his cane. Swiftly, Watson turned, ready to shoot his revolver, though like Houdini himself, the ghostly figure had disappeared out of the room. Watson

gasped, "What in the blazes was that?"

"Why, that was our good friend Professor Moriarty," conveyed Holmes, seemingly unconcerned about his near escape.

"All I saw was a long shiny blade coming down at you," confirmed Watson.

"Yes, my friend just like this one." Holmes turned the handle of his cane and pulled out a long fine sword. "The Professor and I are much alike, even down to these disguises of his. Let us get back to our rooms so I can study them more closely."

"Are you sure he is gone?"

"Yes," Holmes replied, "he wanted what is in this suitcase, so now he will have to find new disguises for Saturday's Magic Show."

Watson laughed, "Don't you mean the 'disappearing' or 'escape artist' show."

"It's all the same, Watson," a straight faced Holmes replied. "Come, let's get back to our rooms." They rushed across the road, entering Holmes' abode and hurried up the stairs. They were both quite pleased to be back in their warm room. The fire was still burning and Mrs Hudson had left them a fresh pot of tea and scones with blackberry jam.

"She is a good old girl," announced Watson, rubbing his hands with delight. Holmes sat in his wingback chair with the suitcase on his lap. Eager, like a child at Christmas time surrounded by their presents, he carefully examined all the items inside the case. Using his large magnifying glass, he went over every item with precision. Watson had a large piece of scone in his mouth, when Holmes said, "Look at these." He held up a set of keys. "This is what Moriarty used in his escape from his goal cell at Scotland Yard. He learned Houdini's swallowing trick, which he apparently mastered. I believe this is what he really came back for tonight."

Watson hastily swallowed some more scone so that he could speak clearly, "Do you think this will affect his plans now?" asked Watson.

Holmes exhaled smoke from his pipe, "Well, he has many friends in the underworld, and he will be able to replace anything he needs. Even the disguises will be easy to replace," concluded Holmes. Watson could tell Holmes was still feeling pleased with himself. After all, he had gotten the chance to investigate a part of his arch-nemesis' private little world, contained inside this suitcase.

Watson sipped some tea and said, "It's going to be very interesting on Saturday night my friend. Very interesting indeed!" Holmes didn't reply, calmly blowing out smoke from his pipe gazing and into the fireplace deep in thought. His eyes gleamed in anticipation.

Chapter 11

Saturday evening finally arrived. Despite some internal trepidation, Holmes and Watson looked very dapper dressed in their top hat and tails. Both men had their revolvers well hidden under the fancy apparel they were wearing. They picked up their walking canes and Holmes pulled his cane's hidden sword blade halfway-out. Sliding it back securely into place with a soft 'shhh-click', he said, "This time Watson I will be ready for him." He didn't have to say his name as Watson would be more than ready for Professor Moriarty as well.

Watson takes his gold watch out of his vest pocket, gently opening it, commented, "Well, it's time Lestrade was here to pick us up." As if on cue, there was a knock at the door. Mrs Hudson showed Lestrade into the room. On seeing Holmes and Watson, her eyes opened wide, and she gasps, "Oh how handsome you all look. You will certainly catch the eyes of all the ladies".

Lestrade, straightened his tie with a big smile, saying, "Well gentlemen, your coach awaits you." Watson looked strangely at Lestrade asking why he was not wearing the anticipated silk top hat instead of his usual bowler hat. "Those blasted things! I keep bumping into the tops of doorways. Don't like them at all." They all laughed, after all it was strange seeing Lestrade in a tuxedo. They said their goodbyes to Mrs Hudson and went downstairs to their coach.

All their fellow detectives were waiting for them. The men were all dressed in top hat and tails, all except Miss Marple, of course. She was wearing a long, blue damask gown with a cream silk shawl around her shoulders. Hercule Poirot was wearing a top hat and tails, though his waistcoat was enlivened, covered in red polka dots. Bulldog Drummond looked immaculate as always. Black always suited him so well. Jules Maigret looked out of place just like Inspector Lestrade. It was not their cup of tea at all. Like la sow's ear trying to look like a silken purse, n'est pas, thought Poirot.

After taking their places on the bus, Holmes asked Lestrade if everything was going to plan. "Yes, I have thirty disguised men and woman in evening wear, (Heaven knows what it will do to my budget), inside the building and I have another hundred outside, hidden, surrounding the whole area."

Holmes nodded, "We want him in, but we don't want him getting out."

"Do you think he will make it inside, Holmes.

"I believe he is already in there," he answered.

Lestrade's face had a look of horror on it, "You mean to say he has gotten past my men already!"

"Yes, and now we set the trap and he must not escape," Holmes' face had an expression of delight on it, just like he was ready for a delicious meal of Moriarty served on a silver platter.

They all disembarked from the coach and stood on the footpath outside the London Palladium. There were glittering crowds of merry makers thronging around. They stopped to look at the large billboard advertising Harry Houdini – 'See it with your own eyes, the World's greatest escape artist! See him escape from the Egyptian Tomb of Death. Many men have died entering this ancient tomb'.

Poirot made a strange, strangling sound that echoed down the footpath. "Houdini, he likes le danger, our good friend", he followed this with another tsk.

Overhearing him, Holmes replied, "Like us all, we play with danger every day." They all nodded in agreement.

A well-dressed man emerged from the theater. "Come," he waved, "I have your seats in the very front row. Mister Houdini told me to take good care of you." They followed him through the beautiful foyer, into the theatre and down the long, red carpet to their front row seats. Maigret walked down the aisle first and sat down, Hugh Drummond following, then Poirot and Miss Marple. Watson took his seat, then Holmes. Inspector Lestrade took his place in the aisle seat.

They all looked up at the stage. A large object covered with a black curtain was positioned in centre stage. With a smile, Bulldog whispered, "You great detectives, no guessing what is under that curtain." They all laughed, even Holmes.

Miss Marple loved Hugh's humor. They were interrupted by an usher calling out, "Peanuts, freshly roasted peanuts, only a penny a bag." The funny looking man who was carrying a tray of peanuts down the aisle, had a large, handlebar mustache. Quickly Lestrade jumped up shouting, "What have we here?" he said looking at the man's mustache. He grabbed him by the arm, "Who do you think you're fooling, look at his fake mustache."

The man struggled, "Inspector, it's me, Constable Appleby in disguise!"

Lestrade's face looked flabbergasted, "Well keep moving," he huffed.

Watson burst into laughter, "Why, you don't even know your own men," he taunted. Watson then noticed the Royal Box with their Majesties, the King and Queen looking down at the stage. Instantly becoming serious, he asked, "Holmes, don't you think it's too dangerous to have the Royal Family here tonight?"

Now it was his turn, Lestrade burst into laughter, "You fool Watson," Lestrade scoffed, "have a closer look. That's not the King, that is Sargeant Wilmot, and the Queen is Constable Katey O'Brian." Lestrade had gotten one back on Watson and Watson did not like it, not one little bit. Both men detested each other, but Watson would have to bide his time get one back on Lestrade.

Holmes' eyes were all over the Palladium watching

everything and everyone, even the most innocuous looking person. He had already identified the policewomen and men in their disguises, all thirty of them. He also knew Moriarty would recognize them too. The trap was set, the trick was to keep him in it.

The house lights dimmed, going out completely, with only the stage lit up. The band started to play 'Auld Lang Syne' and the crowd applauded loudly. Then Houdini and Bess each appeared from opposite wings of the stage, meeting at the centre, holding each other's hands. The crowd applauded even louder. Houdini, dressed in his black tuxedo looked immaculate. Bess dressed in a shimmering aqua, body-hugging gown, looked stunning. The audience were in awe of this famous couple, greeting them with smiles of adoration. They both looked up at the Royal Box and bowed to the King and Queen. The Royal couple graciously nodded and smiled. The audience again applauded with vigor and excitement.

Lestrade looked at Watson with a sneering smile, "If they only knew," he whispered.

Watson's hand tightened around his walking cane, but quietly Holmes intervened, "Now gentlemen, we must have our wits about us. We don't have time for distractions. Moriarty can strike at any moment so we must be ready."

Their attention was refocused by Houdini's deep voice. With a flourish of his arms he said, "Now, my Lords, Ladies and Gentlemen, I would like you to all see my Egyptian

Tomb of Death! Bess pulled aside the large black curtain and there it was. All eyes stared in astonishment at the dark, evil-looking artifact. Aghast, the crowd's gasps echoed around the Palladium.

"Blimey," cried Lestrade, "you would never get me in that thing!" The Death Chamber was about eight feet tall and four feet wide. It stood upright with a large, coffin-like door. Carved on the door was a sculpture of a Mummied King, wrapped in bandages. "Blimey," Lestrade repeated aghast, "he was a tall blighter, wasn't he?"

Holmes replied that it was the custom for deceased Pharaohs to take many of their prized possessions into the nether world with them, so they needed a large tomb. "It's all a bit creepy for me," replied Lestrade. "Give me an Anglican cemetery any day."

All the other detectives looked on, watching and assessing everything and everyone. To their surprise Houdini invited all of the great detectives up onto stage to help with his escape performance. The crowd applauded on seeing all these famous detectives together. Houdini had to wave to the applauding crowd to quiet down. Finally, the room was silent. "You must remember I am the star here tonight," he quipped. The room fell into laughter and cheers. Harry Houdini bowed to his audience with a big appreciative smile.

"Now gentlemen," he instructed, holding out a pair of handcuffs, "I want Doctor Watson to put these onto my wrists and for all of you to make sure they are secure."

Lestrade whispered, "Well, we know how he does this little trick, don't we?"

Watson gave Lestrade a disgusted look as they all checked the handcuffs. They all gave their approval that they were secured and locked. Houdini then opened the coffin door and entered. As the door was so high, he did not have to duck his head. Standing inside the coffin he had them chain his legs and then, to the audience's horror, he had them put a strait jacket onto him. Lestrade grinned, "Blimey, how is he going to get out of this lot."

Bess then waved to the audience and closed the coffin door with a dull thud. She then pulled the black curtain back around the Chamber of Death. Bess held up an hourglass, partially filled with sand. Loudly she announced, "He only has five minutes to free himself and to be standing beside me, right here," pointing to the very spot beside her.

The crowd applauded with excitement and even the great detectives watched in wonder. Watching the sand fall with every second, every minute seeming to take forever. Then finally the last speck of sand fell hitting the bottom of the glass. The coffin door flew open, and everyone froze in shock. For standing next Bess stood Professor Moriarty dressed in a black tuxedo and top hat. He was undisguised. Taking off his top hat he waved to the crowd and turning to the great detectives he tilted his hat to them. Looking into Holmes' eyes

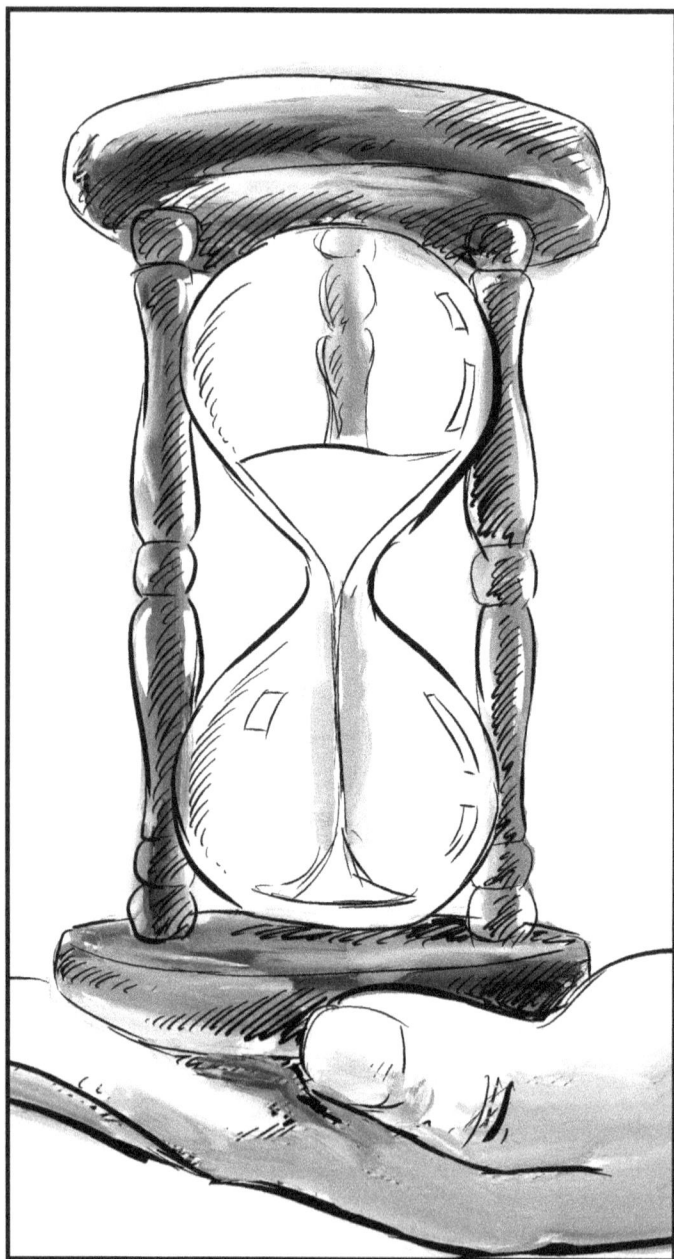

with an arrogant gleam, he turned and disappeared back into the Chamber of Death, slamming the door shut behind him. Holmes ran over trying to open it, but it was impossible. Bess started to cry, "Oh Harry, oh Harry, what has happened to you."

On que, the door opened and out walked Harry Houdini. The crowd roared with excitement, not realizing this was no magic trick. Houdini fell into his wife's arms, Doctor Watson helping to hold him on his feet. Lestrade shouted, "He will never escape from here."

Holmes looked into Lestrade's eyes, saying, "It's too late. A new game has just begun gentlemen."

Chapter 12

The next morning a sleepy Watson was surprised to find Holmes dressed in his frockcoat and wearing his deerstalker. He looked surprisingly cheerful despite what had transpired the previous night. "Where are we off to, he asked.

"Ahh, Watson we will be returning to the Palladium. I want to investigate that Egyptian tomb."

"Holmes! You are not going inside that wretched thing. Are you?"

Putting up his hand to quieten Watson's dismay he said, "Say no more. It must be done. And it will be done."

Picking up their walking canes they headed for London's Palladium Theatre. As it was Sunday morning there were few passers-by. On arrival they were greeted by the Caretaker. "Mister Holmes, what can I do for you this morning? There are no performances scheduled today," he asked.

"I want to have a look at the Egyptian Tomb. I imagine that it will still be on the stage," he answered.

The Caretaker looked from one man to the other in shock, "What, are you are going inside that thing?" he cried in dismay.

Homes entered the Theatre, and climbed the stairs to the stage. The Tomb was still in place. Nothing had been moved. He walked over to the Tomb, opened the door and climbed

Mister Holmes,

Kindly meet me at midnight tonight on the Tower Bridge. Come alone. We will finish it for once and for all. Only one of will survive.

carefully inside. Thankfully for the men's nerves he didn't shut the door. Watson and the Caretaker stood back, watching nervously, and waited for him to come back out. It took a good five minutes until he exited and they were both very relieved as they had feared the worst. Holmes had big smile on his face and he was holding an envelope. "Come, Watson," he ordered, "we have work to do."

The Caretaker scratched his head as they a walked off. "They're right you know. Those Nobs are different to normal folk."

Back at Baker Street Holmes read the message aloud to Watson. "Mister Holmes, kindly meet me at midnight tonight on Tower Bridge. Come alone. We will finish it for once and for all. Only one of us will survive."

"No!" Watson cried, "I am coming too!"

"No!" answered Holmes. "It's him and I. I am going to finish this game tonight. As he says, for once and for all."

At 11.15 pm Watson watched his friend walk out the door with a determined step. He had given Holmes his word that he wouldn't follow him. This was a promise that he couldn't possibly keep. After waiting thirty minutes Watson started for Tower Bridge, almost running to catch Holmes. On reaching the Bridge the fog was so thick it blanketed everything. Visibility was virtually non-existent. Watson was dismayed to hear the sound of sword blades clashing in the darkness.

Holmes and Moriarty were engaged in a furious sword

fight on the Tower Bridge. They were totally engrossed. Both men were excellent swordsmen. They had crossed blades before and were fairly evenly matched. As Watson drew nearer, he heard Moriarty scream as Holmes sword went right through his side in a classic manoeuvre that he surprisingly failed to block. "If I die, you die! I will take you with me to hell," he bellowed. Grabbing Holmes' shoulder, he tried to pull him off the bridge as Moriarty fell backwards towards the water. Like Houdini's magic trick, Holmes managed to slip out of his frockcoat and quickly jumped aside. Moriarty fell backwards into the River Thames clutching the coat in vain, Holmes' sword was still sticking through his side. He screamed all the way down to the water, the deep, black, cold black water. "Damn you Holmes."

Moriarty's body was never found. A few weeks later Watson asked, "Do you think he is gone for good"

"We will have to wait and see, won't we?" a smiling Holmes answered.

www.ingramcontent.com/pod-product-compliance
Lightning Source LLC
Chambersburg PA
CBHW021837020426
42334CB00014B/668